# Bee Coloring Book

BY KID KONGO



ISBN: 10: 1533014841
ISBN-13: 978-1533014849

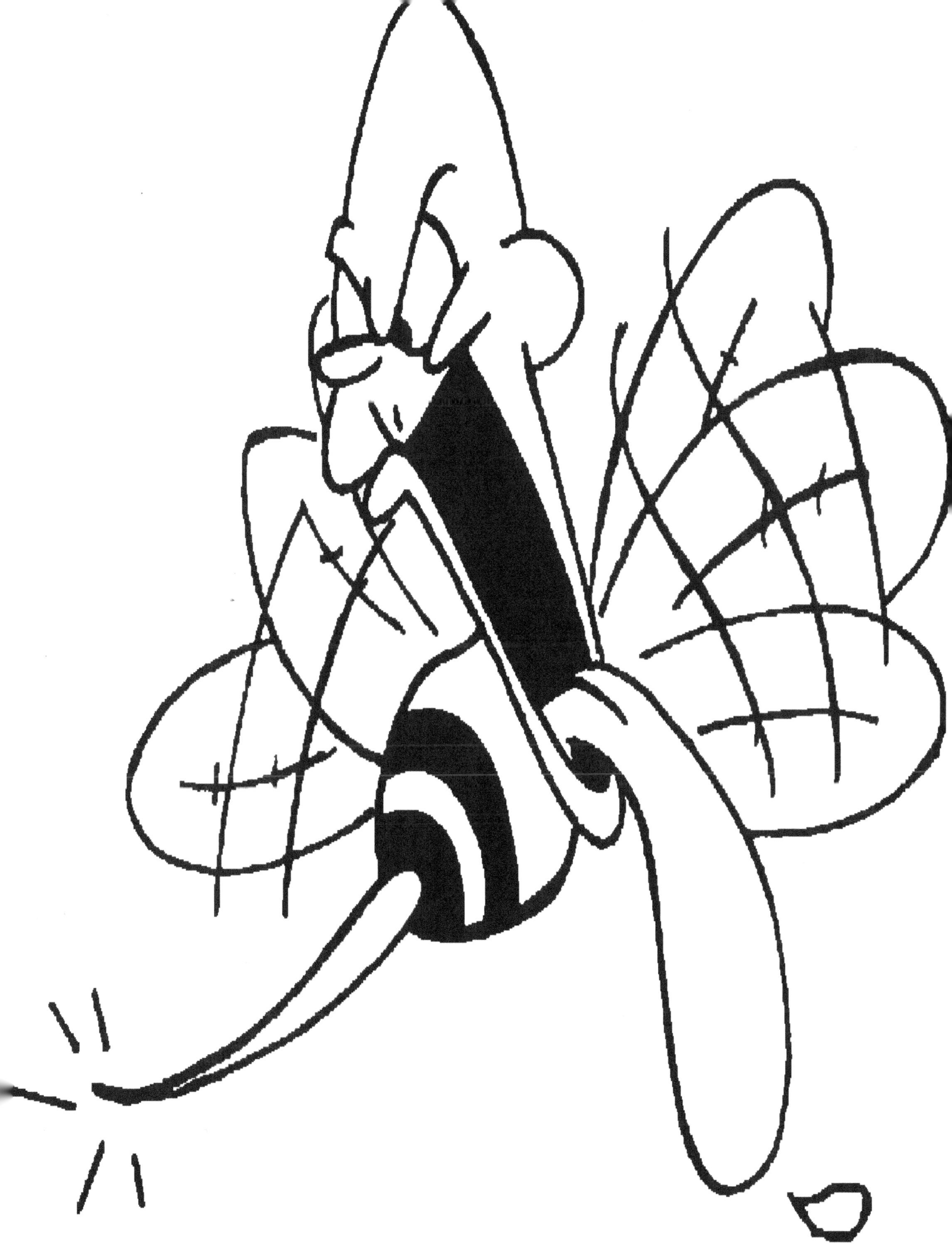

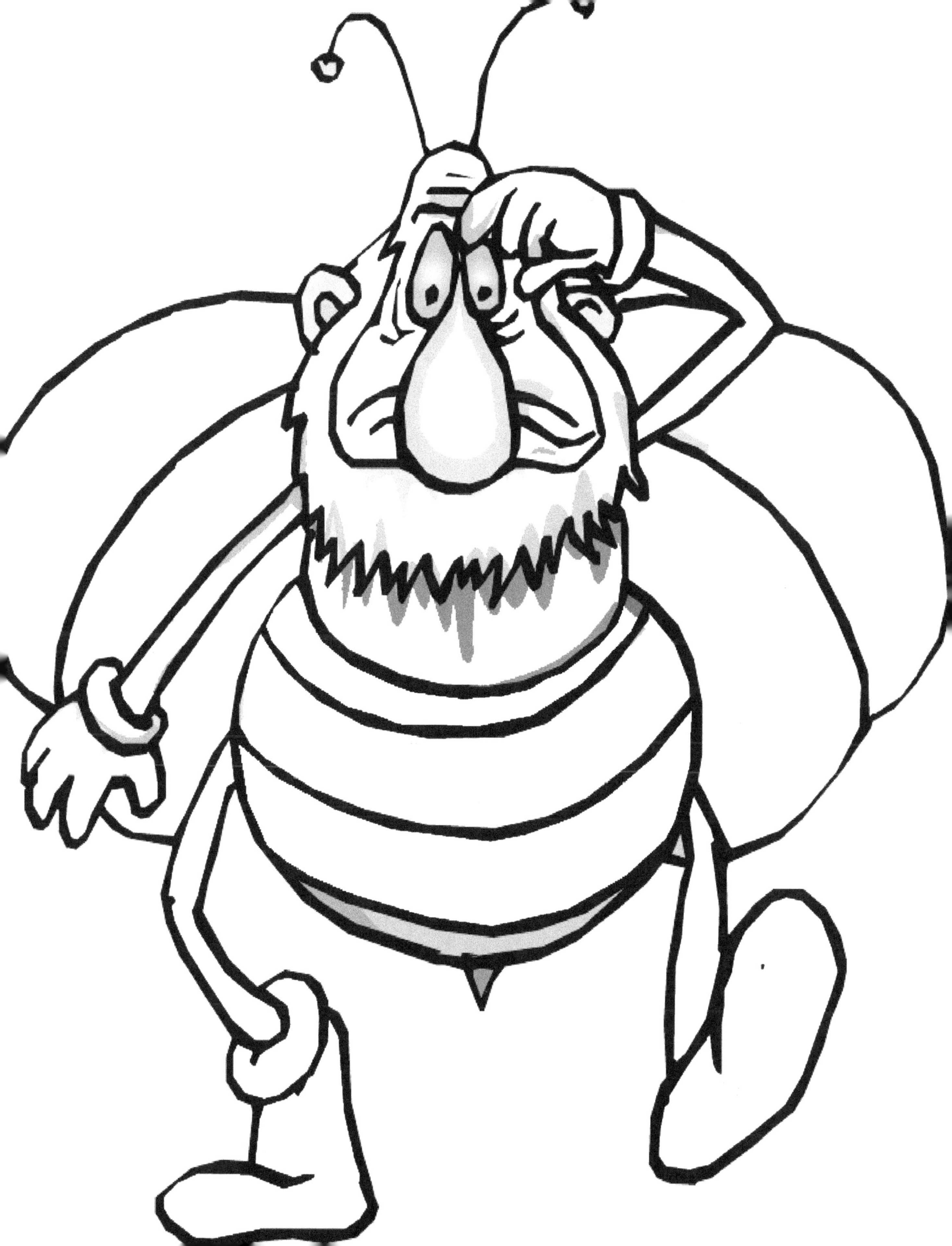

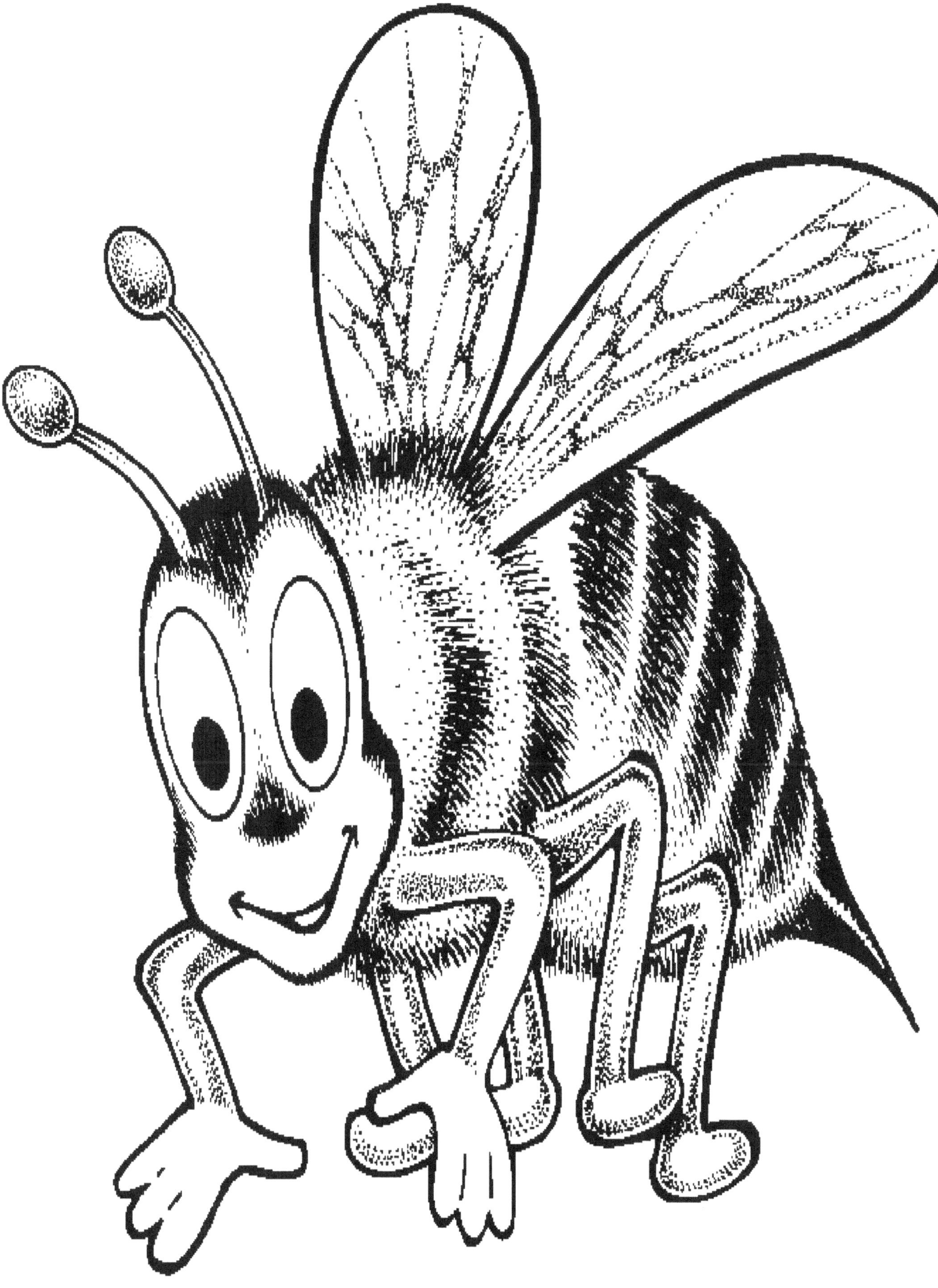

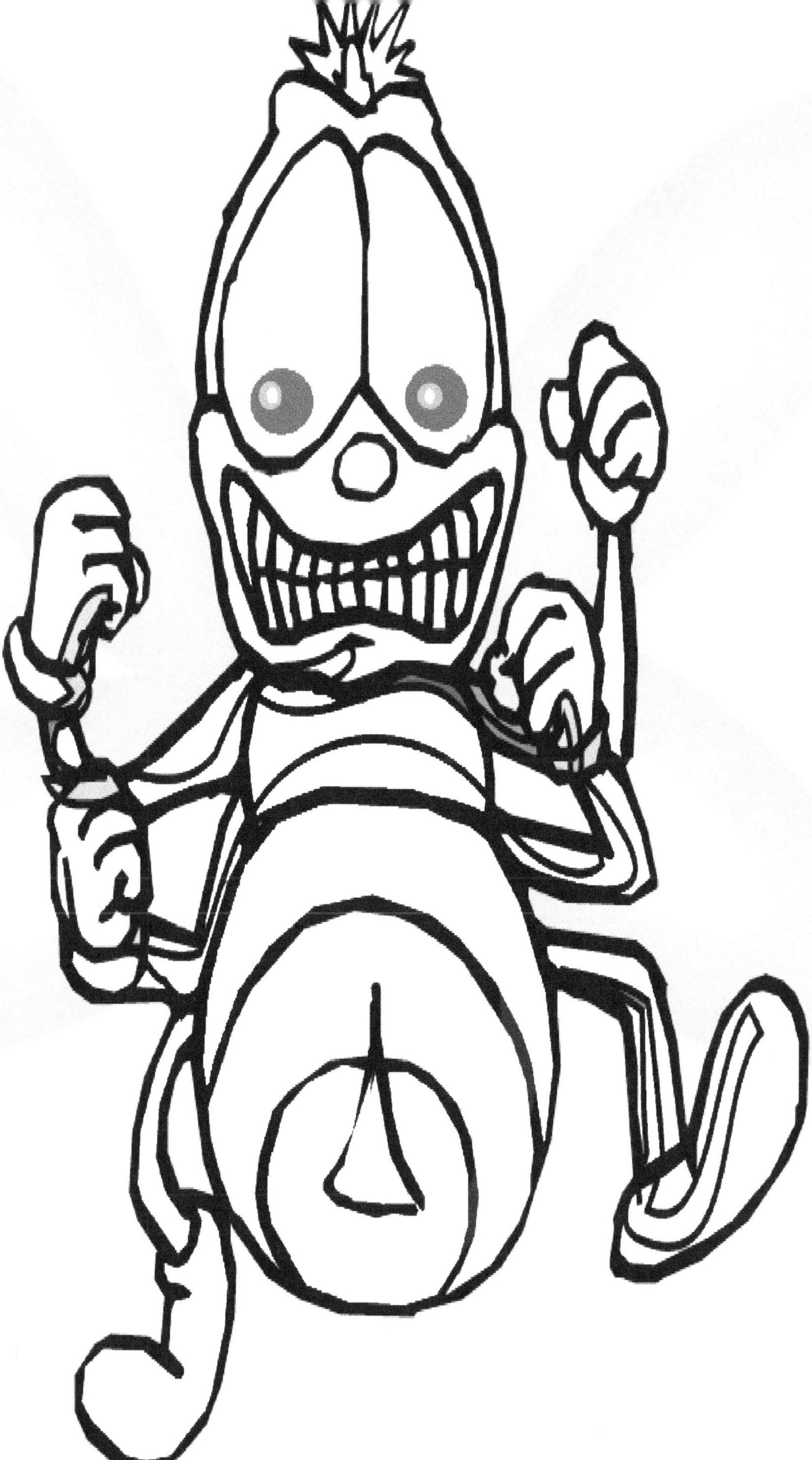

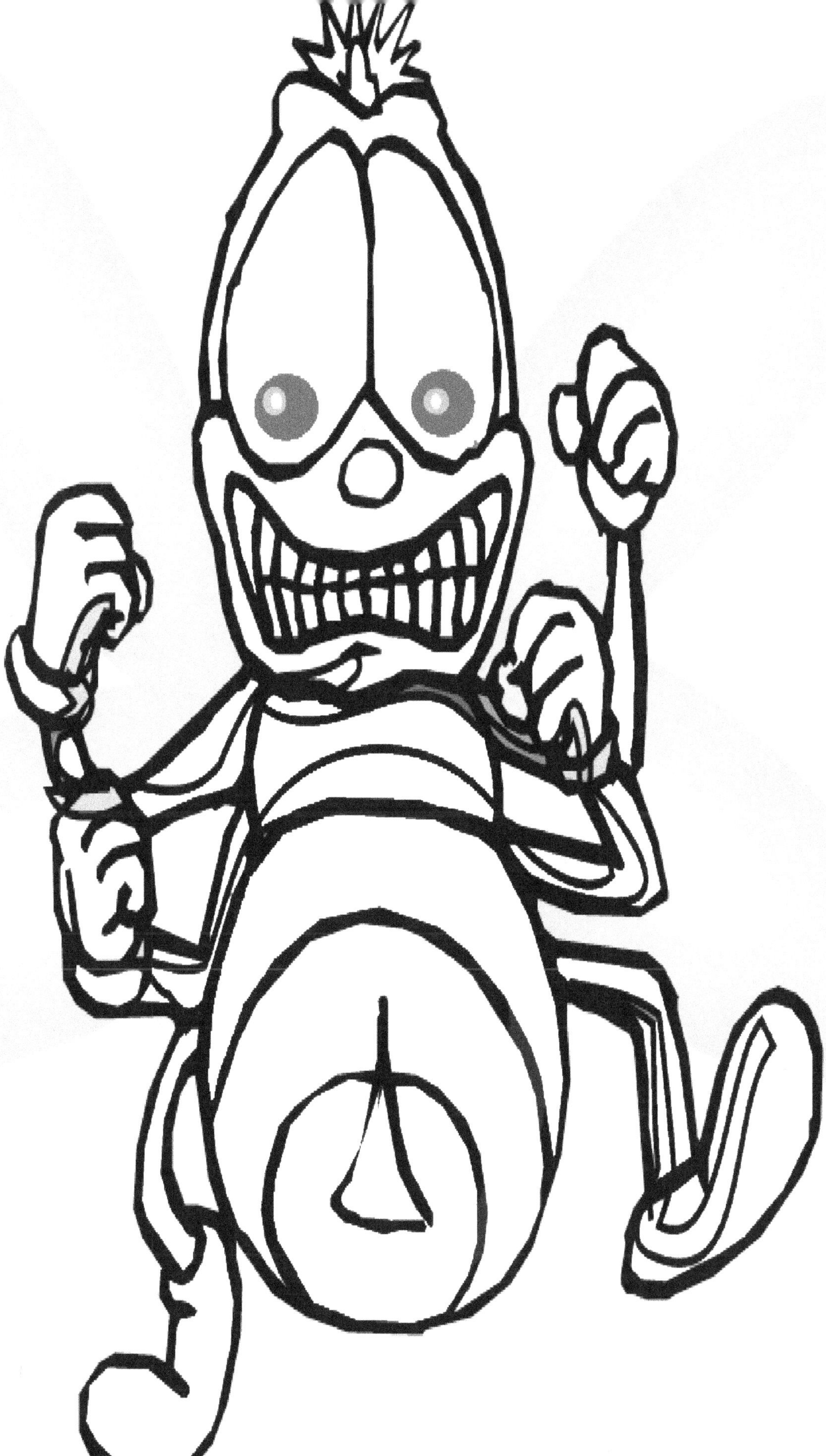

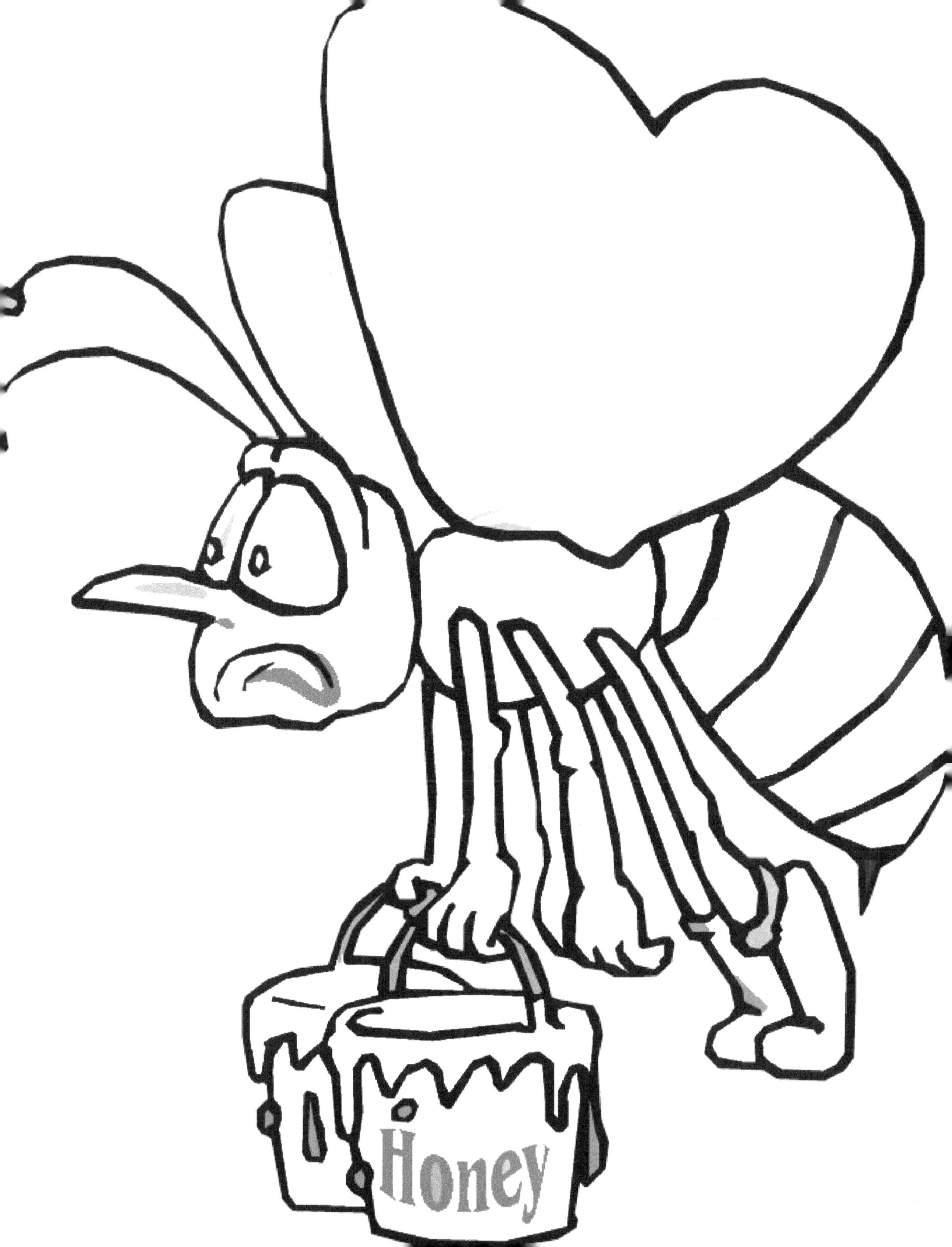
Honey

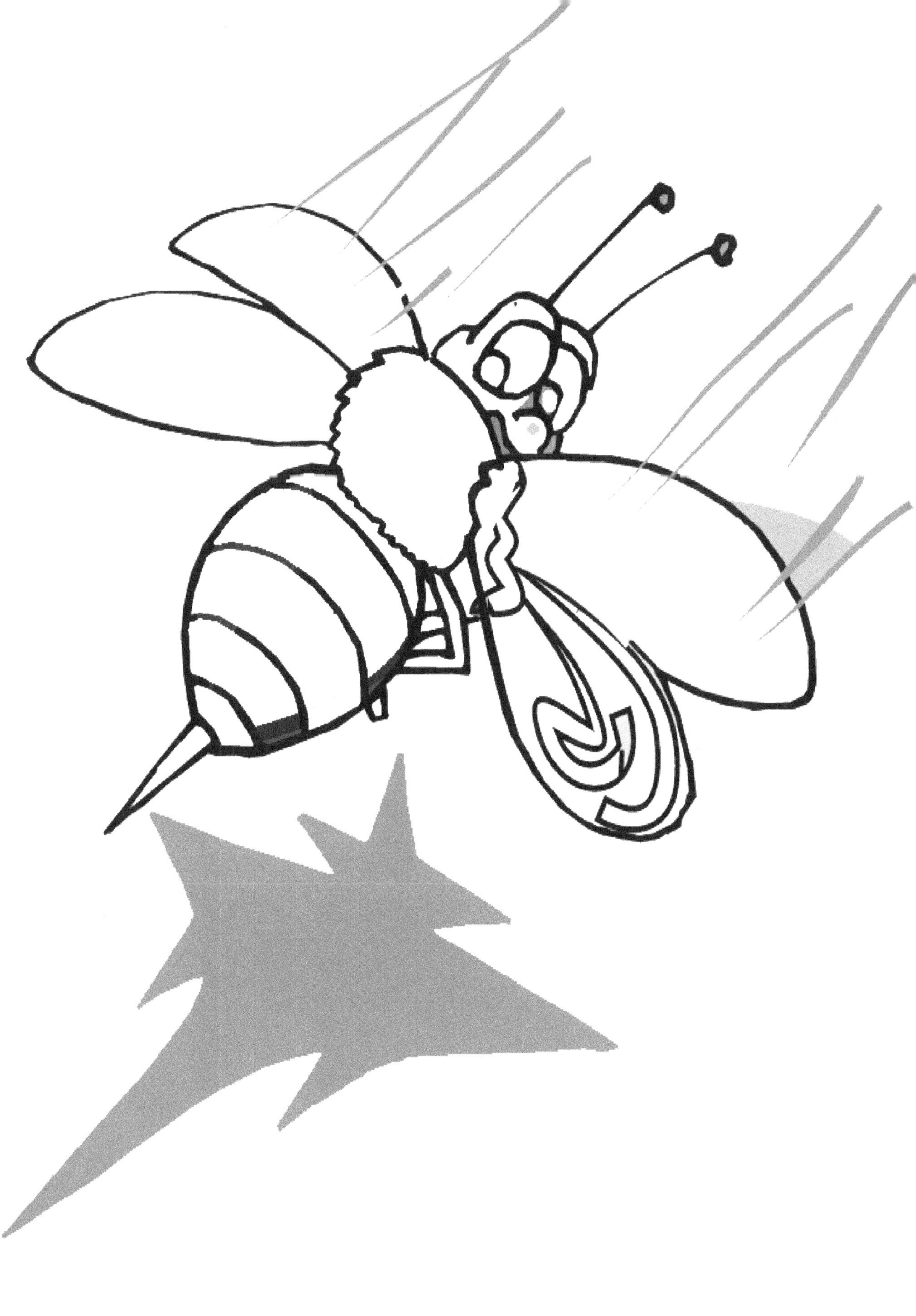

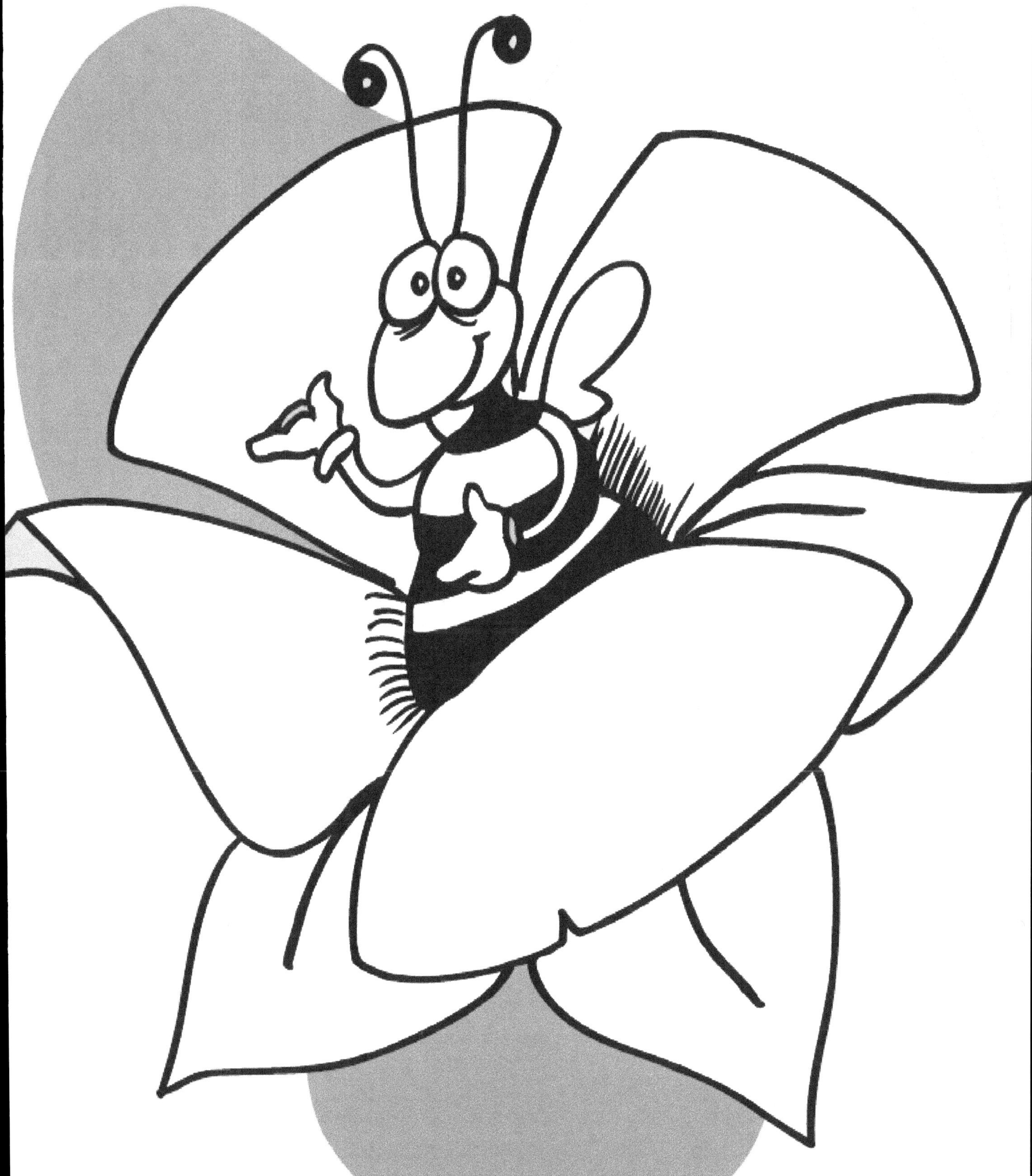

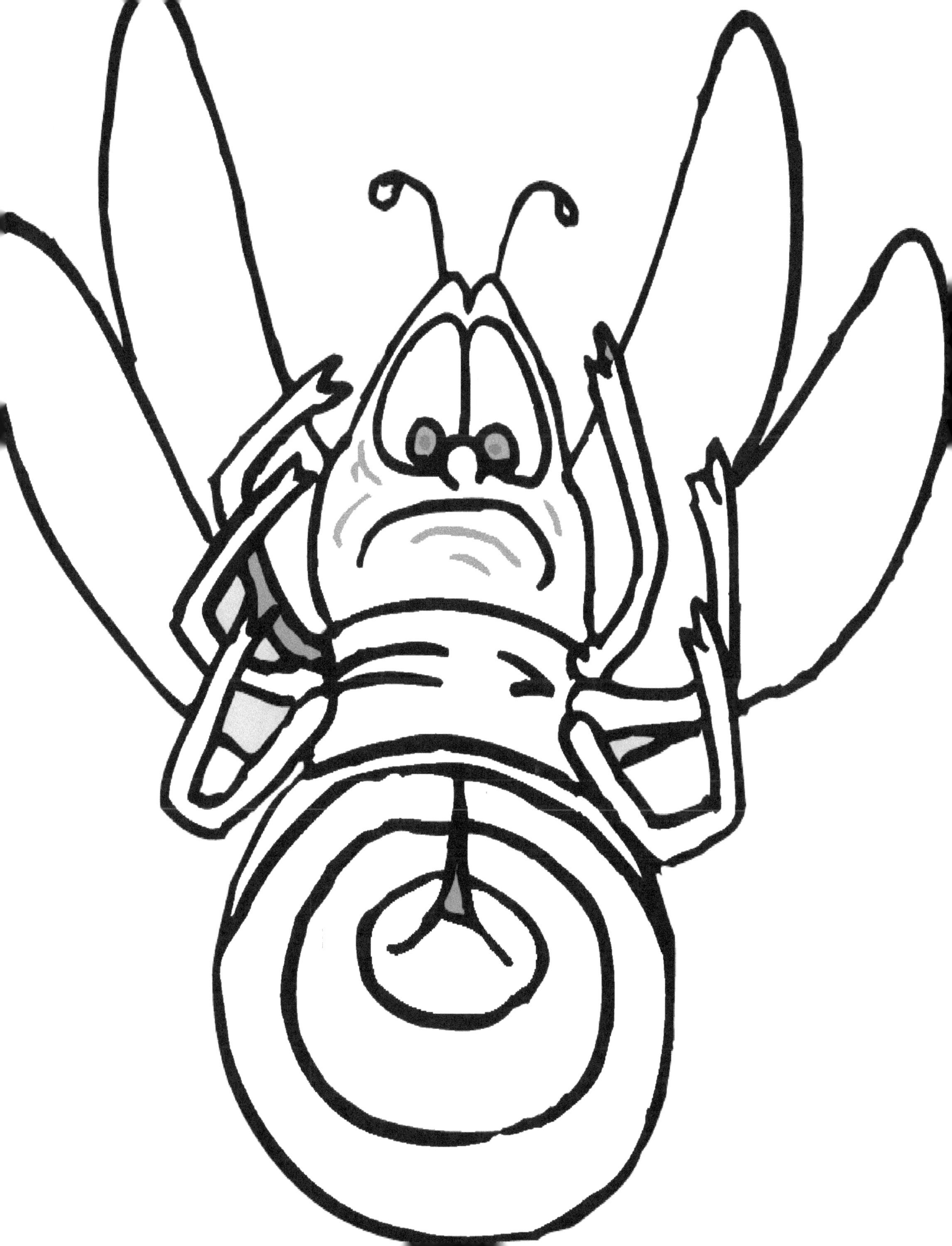

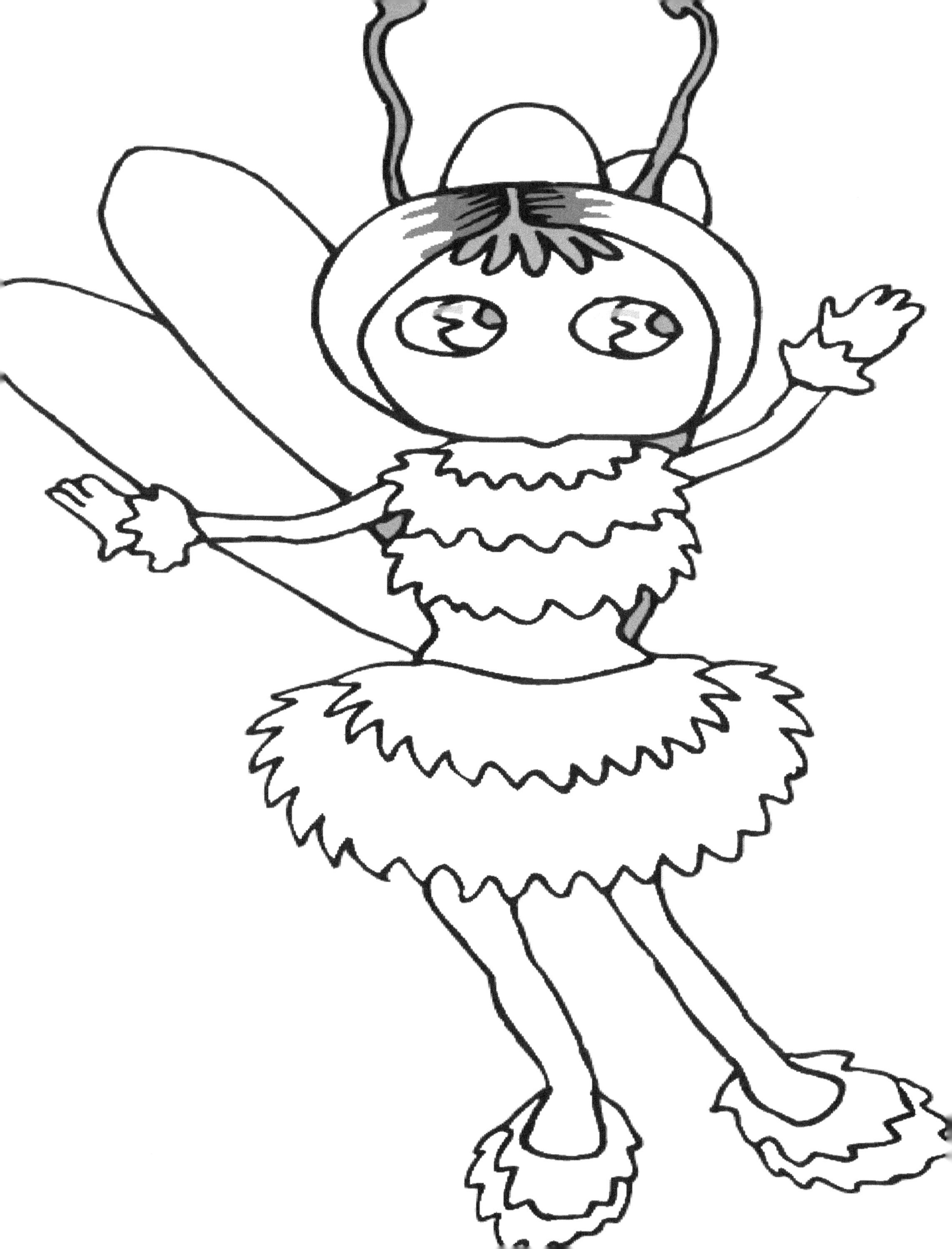

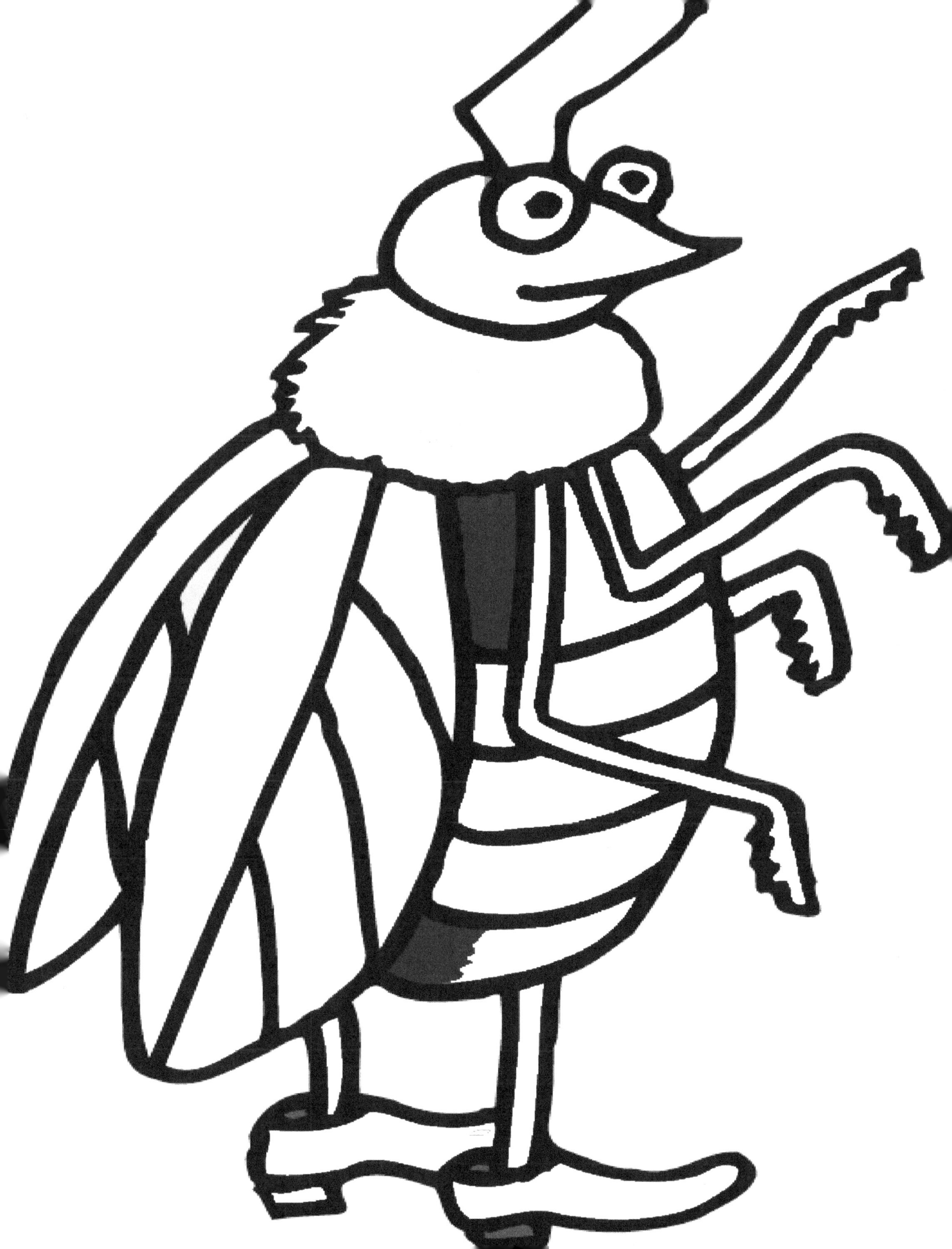

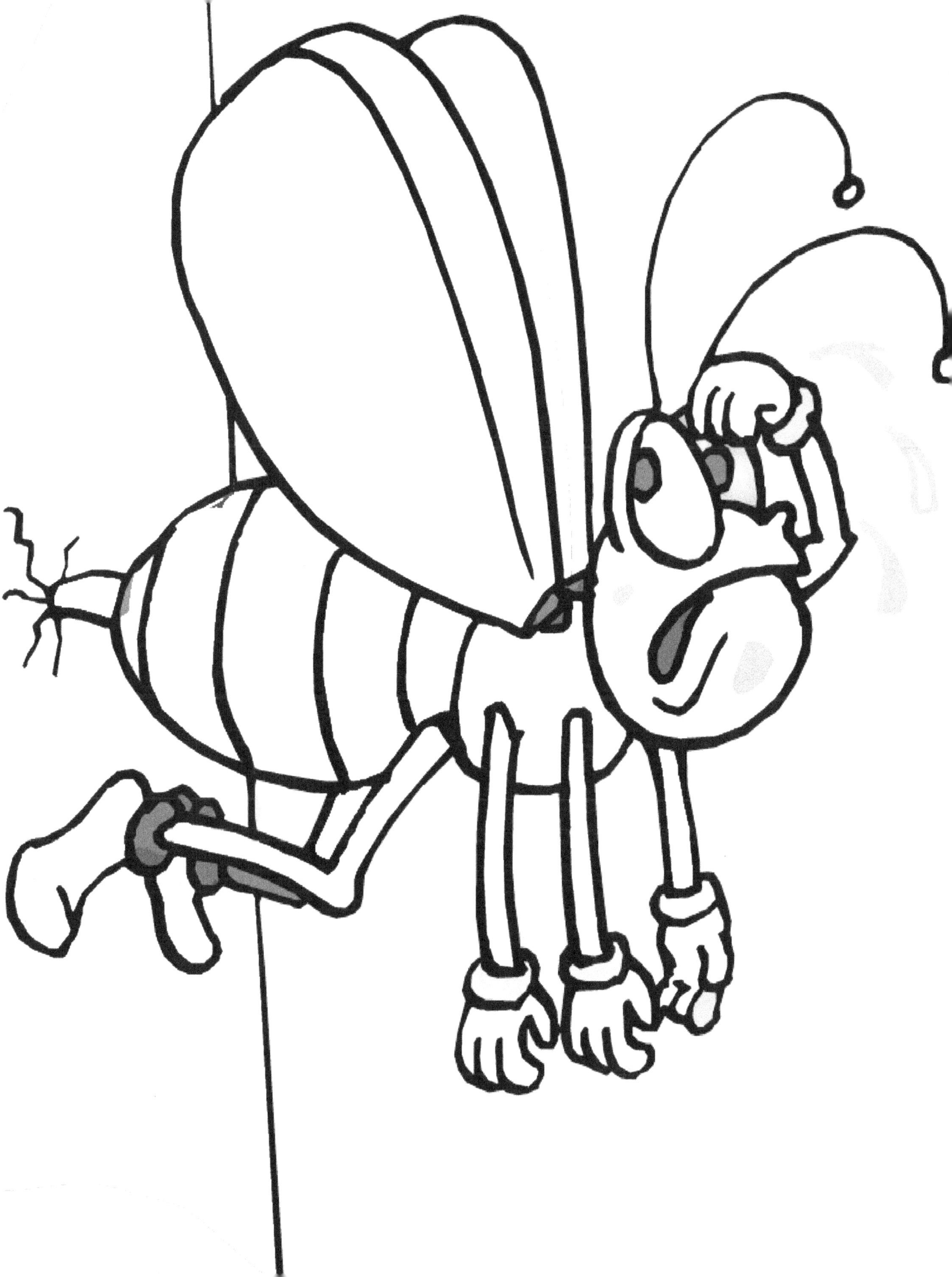

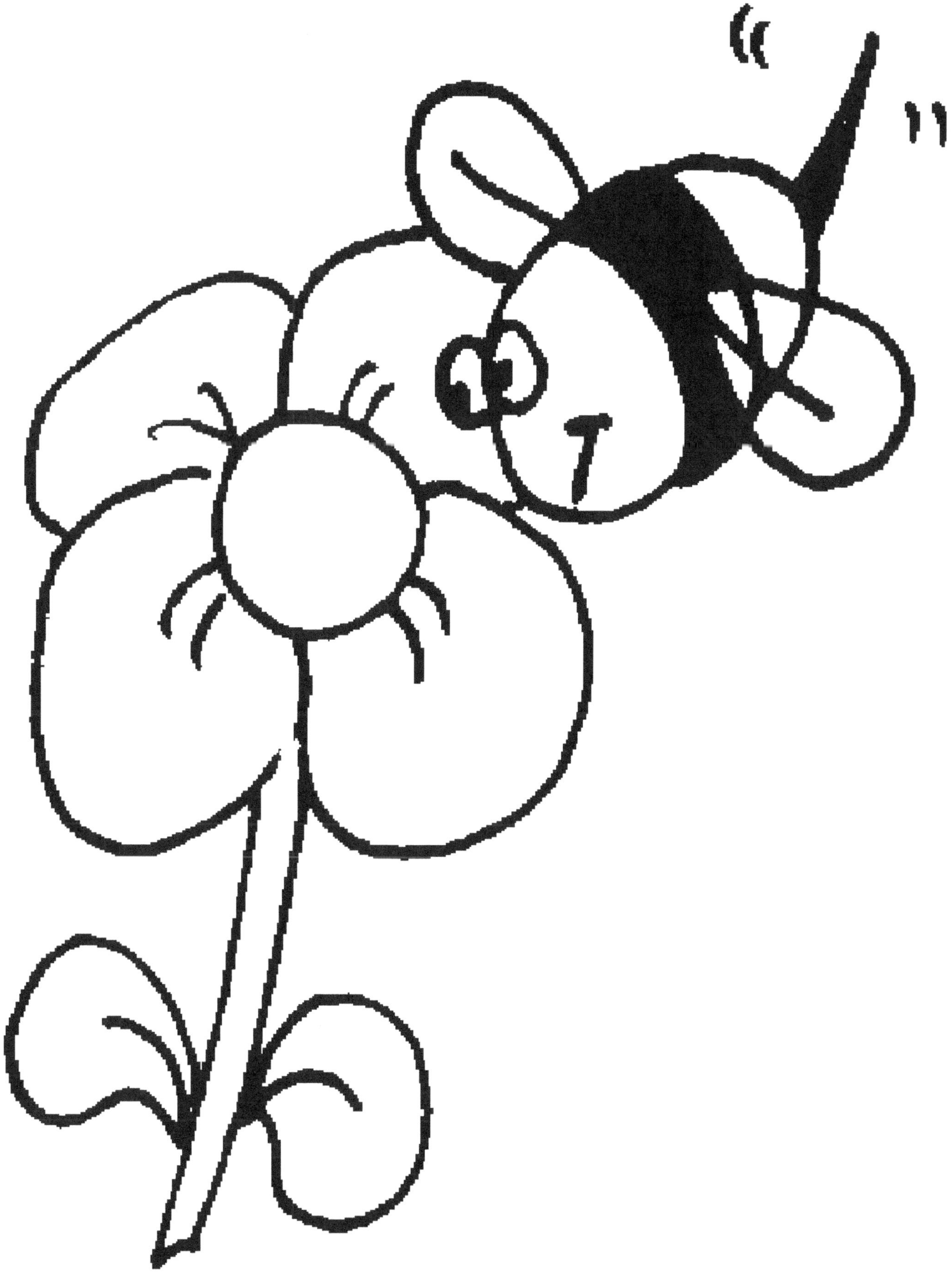

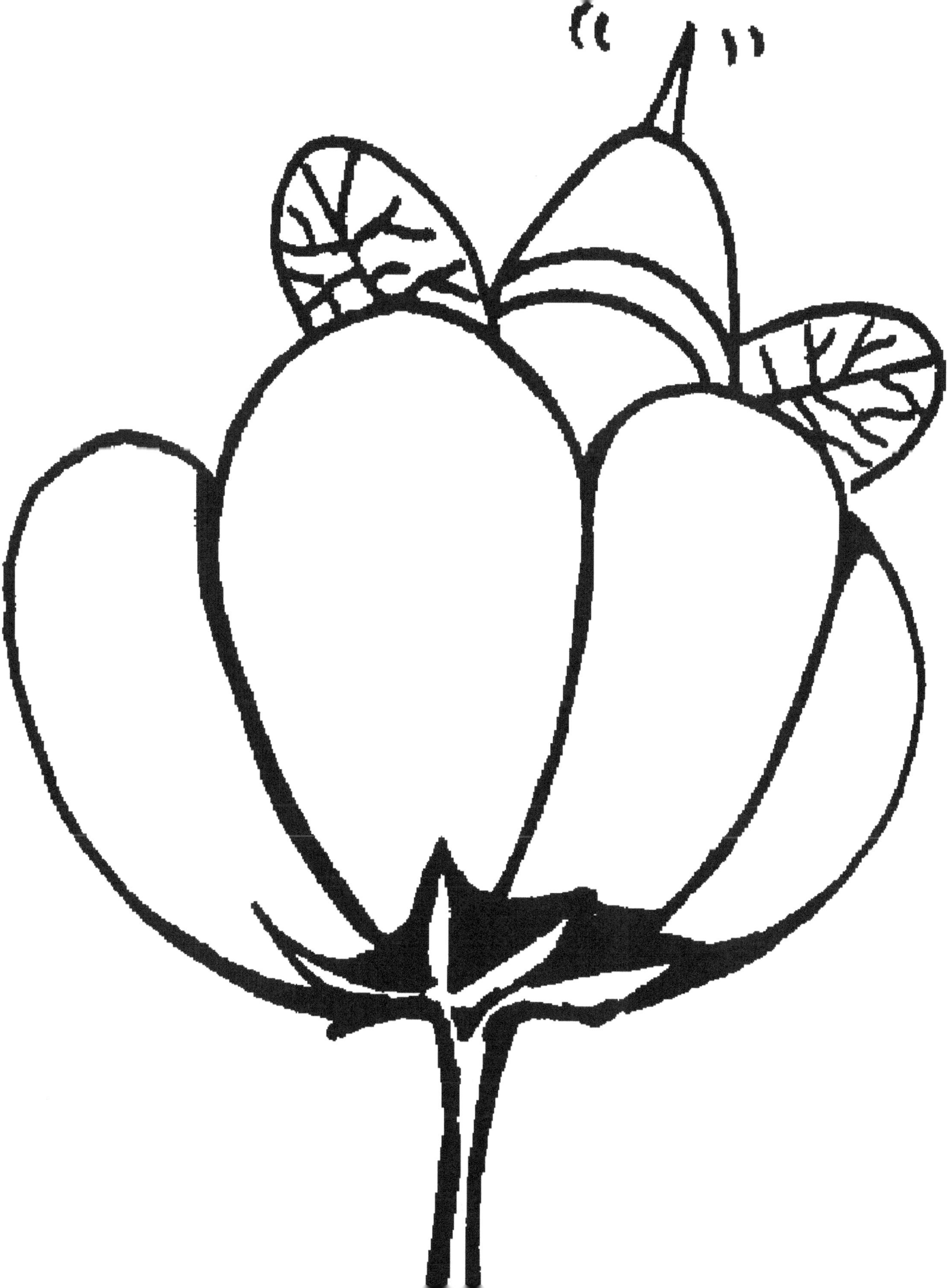

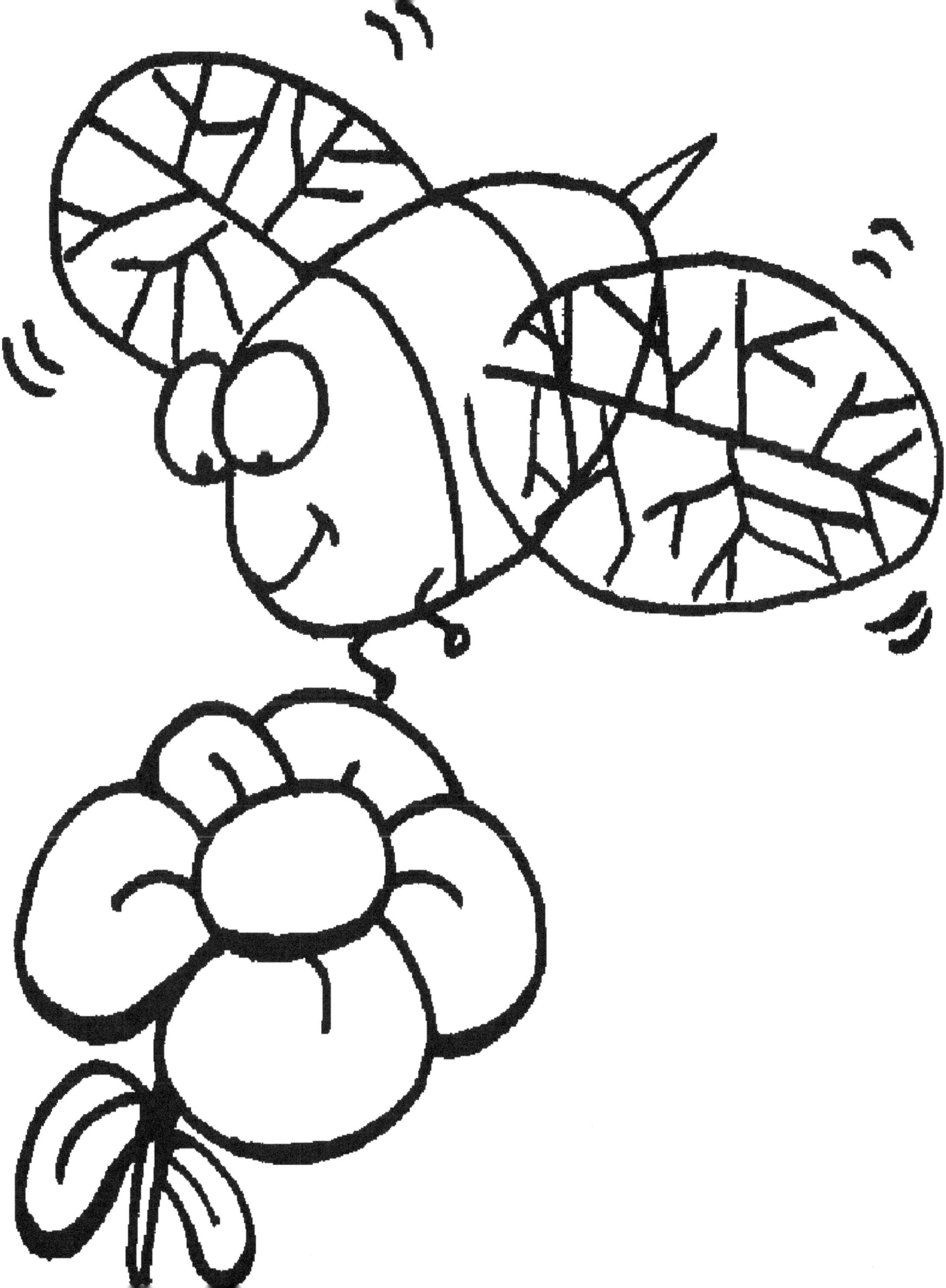

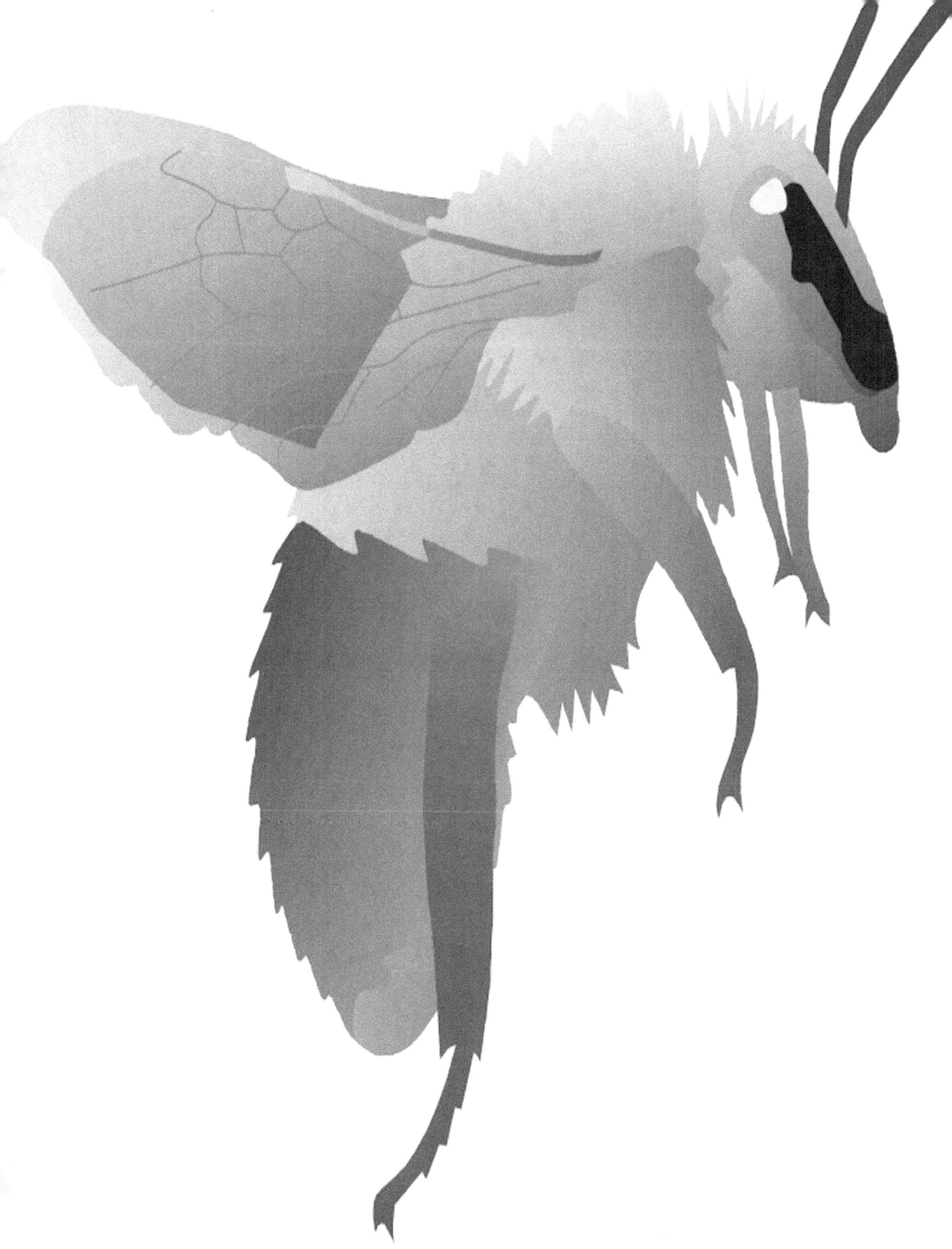

www.ingramcontent.com/pod-product-compliance
Lightning Source LLC
Chambersburg PA
CBHW081140280526
45787CB00007B/3158
* 9 7 8 1 5 3 3 0 1 4 8 4 9 *